INNOVATIVE ART QUILTS FROM CALIFORNIA AND NEVADA

On The Fringe

Premier venue

Texas Quilt Museum
140 W Colorado Street
La Grange, Texas 78945
www.texasquiltmuseum.org

June 30 - September 25, 2016

Traveling to

Harrington Art Gallery
4444 Railroad Avenue
Pleasanton, California 94566
www.firehousearts.org

March 9 - April 15, 2017

SAQA™
Studio **Art** Quilt Associates

www.saqa.com
www.saqa-norcal.blogspot.com

SAQA was founded in 1989 as a non-profit organization whose mission is to promote the art quilt through education, exhibitions, professional development, documentation and publications.

Forward

This show is as far from the status quo as possible, with the unique flavor of the West coast, long known for its creativity and innovation. Our artists from the Northern California/Northern Nevada Region of the Studio Art Quilt Associates (SAQA) use diverse materials and a variety of surface design techniques, such as photography, painting, dyeing, stitch resist, screen printing and other mixed media. Whether the work is representational or abstract. *On the Fringe* showcases the exciting art quilts and expanding quilt vocabulary of our most innovative creators.

Our only guideline from SAQA is the art quilt be "a creative visual work that is layered and stitched or that references this form of stitched layered structure." Our goal for this show is to take the versatility of the textile medium and create fresh approaches in our artwork. Textiles can be pliable or firm, smooth or textural, 2-dimensional or 3-dimensional, sheer or opaque, representational or abstract. Textiles can stand on their own or work well with other mediums. The theme provided a wonderful opportunity for our artists to try out new techniques or to utilize known techniques in new ways. Each artist interpreted the theme of being "on the fringe" in her own way and focused on the content of the artwork.

We would like to thank all of our artists for submitting work for the show and the support of our total membership for our shows. A special thank you goes to our Juror and Texas Quilt Museum curator, Dr. Sandra Sider, for her vision, her considered selections and insightful captions for each selection, and her remarkable Juror's Statement.

Curatorial team: Patricia Porter, Denise Oyama Miller, Gail Sims

Juror's Statement

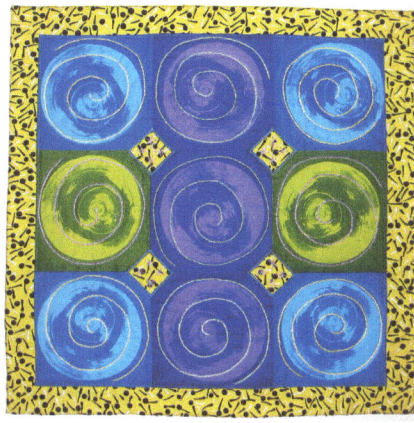

Sandra Sider
"3 x 3 Wine Glasses"
22" x 22"

This exhibition of twenty art quilts exemplifies some of the more interesting work being done today by members of Studio Art Quilt Associates (SAQA) who belong to the northern California and northern Nevada regional group.

Premiering in summer of 2016 at the Texas Quilt Museum, *On the Fringe* brings us the unique character of the West Coast in a variety of diverse materials, subjects, and surface design techniques. Connotations of "fringe" include areas on and near the Pacific Rim, looking toward Asia; the geography and topography of California and Nevada as western limits of the continental United States; and, artists pushing the boundaries of their medium, in the spirit of "fringe" festivals worldwide where art challenges and provokes the imagination.

Three artists in the exhibition display Asian influences-Margaret Fabrizio, Rickie Seifried (a Nevada artist), and Gail Sims. Fabrizio incorporates images of Shiva, one of the main three Hindu deities, the god of destruction who destroys the world for it to be recreated and renewed, an appropriate association for those who make quilts by cutting apart and reassembling fabric. Enso II by Seifried honors the Japanese symbol of a Zen perfect circle, sacred and infinite, in gestural style. Shinrin Yoku, or "forest bathing" practiced in Japan to instill tranquility, appeals to Sims, who recalls fondly her childhood visits to the Japanese Garden in the Brooklyn Botanical Garden.

Five artists interpret imagery and events in nature--Giny Dixon, Joan Dyer, Denise Oyama Miller, Nancy Ryan (the other Nevada artist in this exhibition), and Gail Sims, with two works in the show. Dyer, Miller, and Ryan address the forests of California with their original imagery, while both Dixon and Sims deal with natural processes in a conceptual manner. Dixon documents the Sierra snowpack, important for the water supply, and Sims celebrates the promise of spring.

Maria Billings, the other artist exhibiting two quilts, demonstrates how the "fringe" theme expands the definition of "art quilt." Both her quilts incorporate unorthodox materials that complement her compositions. The subjects treated by other artists in the exhibition also demanded thought and ingenuity: Sharon Rossi's modular structure, Ann Grundler's vivid shibori, Jennifer Landau's serendipitous felting, Karen Balos's sassy irregular contours, Martha Wolfe's bicycle, Nancy Bardach's defragging, Karin Lusnak's extreme Log Cabin, Cathy Miranker's homage to Delaunay, and Kathy Grady's neo-traditional coffee bags. Lin Schiffner's Photosynthesis 1.0 features actual fringe in the most conceptual piece of the show.

On the Fringe indicates how effectively Studio Art Quilt Associates (founded 1989) has nurtured and supported its members, now more than 3400 strong. Art quilts have become a salient aspect of contemporary art, valued by museums and collectors, and attracting many thousands of viewers worldwide to similar exhibitions.

Dr. Sandra Sider
Curator, Texas Quilt Museum

SAQA Past President

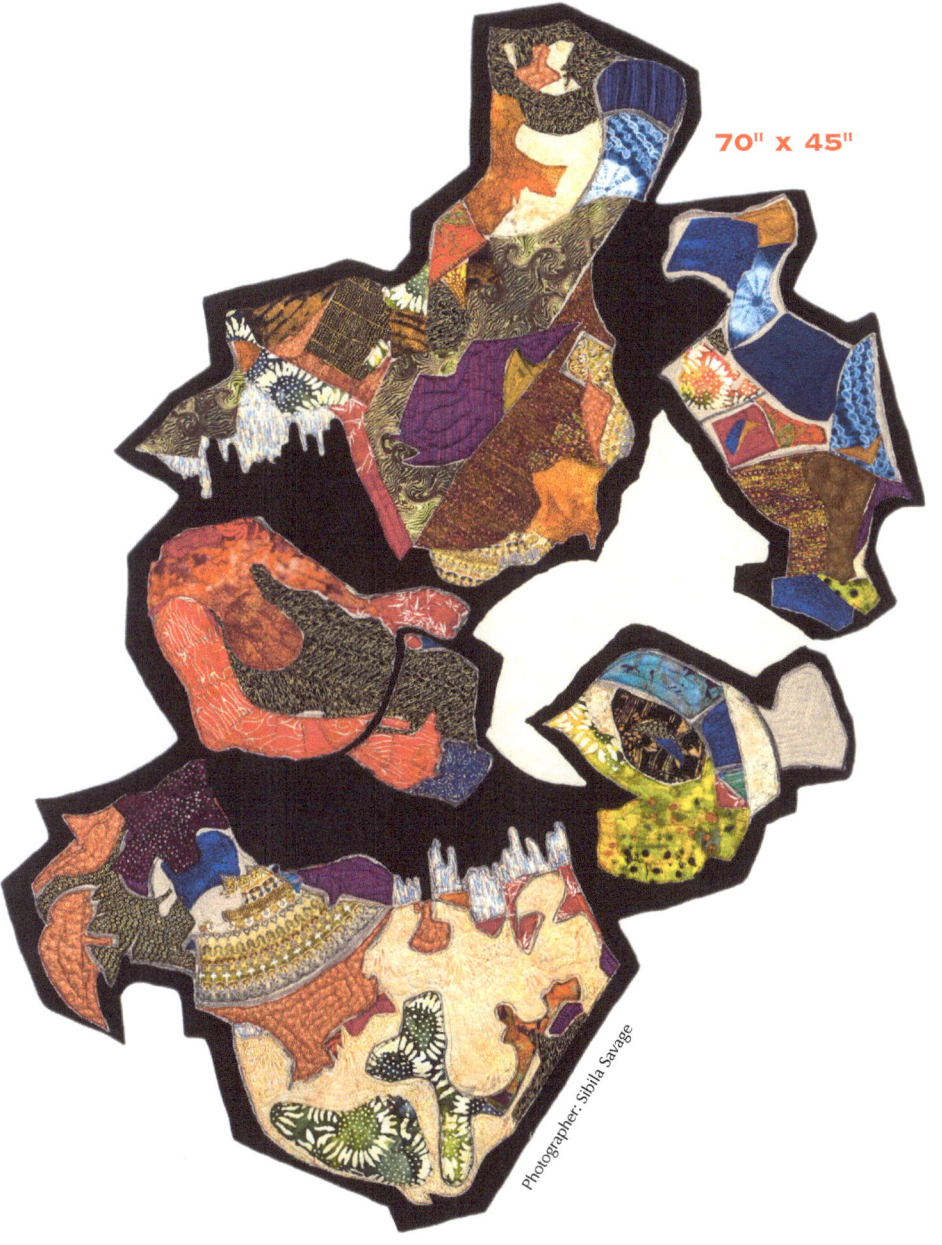

70" x 45"

Photographer: Sibila Savage

Inpired by the shaped paintings of Elizabeth Murray and Frank Stella that push beyond a rectangular format, Balos left her own comfort zone while assembling this quilt. Using mostly fabrics given to her by California quilt artist Alice Beasley, she applied upholstery textiles and felt to create vibrant texture and dynamic contours.

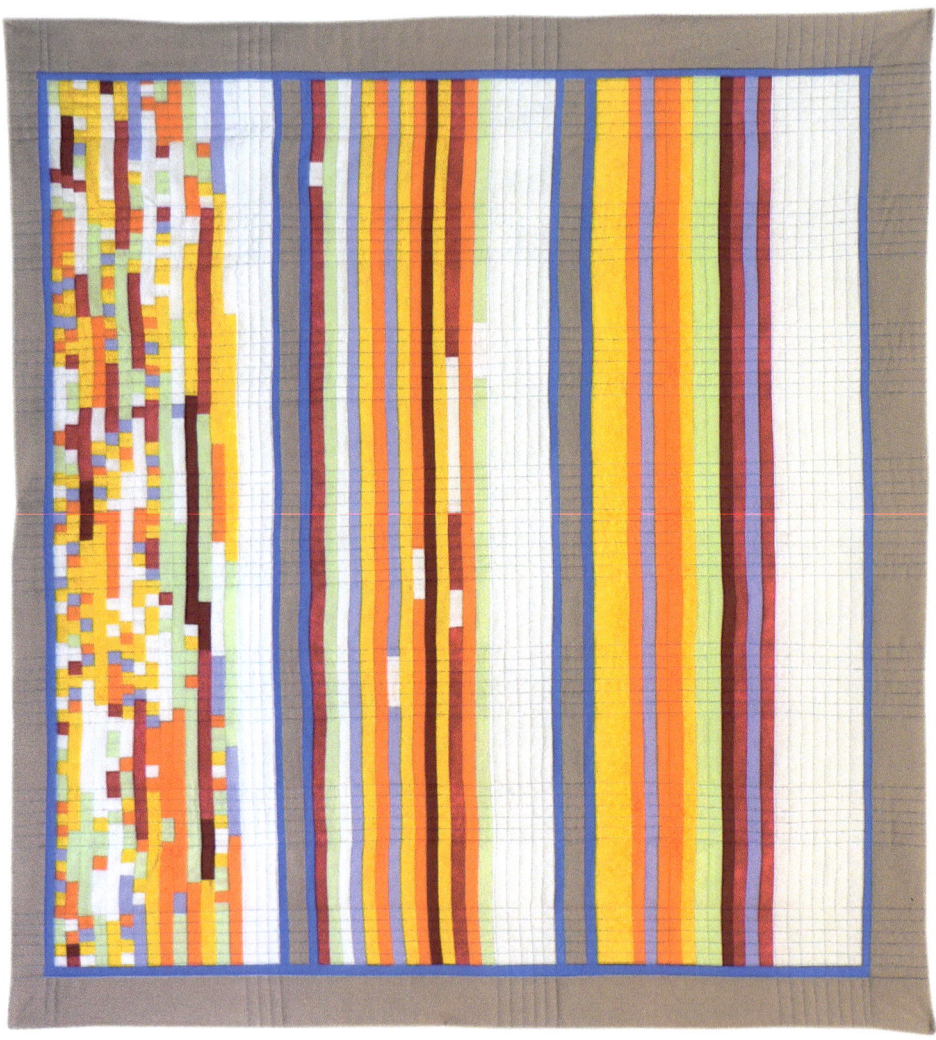

NANCY BARDACH "DEFRAGGING: A TIME-LAPSE VIEW"

Conceptual thinking is the hallmark of Nancy Bardach's art, and here she captured the motion of a computer monitor whose hard disk is being defragged. Our eye moves from left to right, from the chaotic fragments of clutter to pure, straight lines of clarity. We can imagine Bardach sitting in front of her monitor, watching the defrag process, and then suddenly inspired. Note how the quilting adds a pleasing counter-rhythm to the surface.

MARIA BILLINGS "BUBBLE BATH"

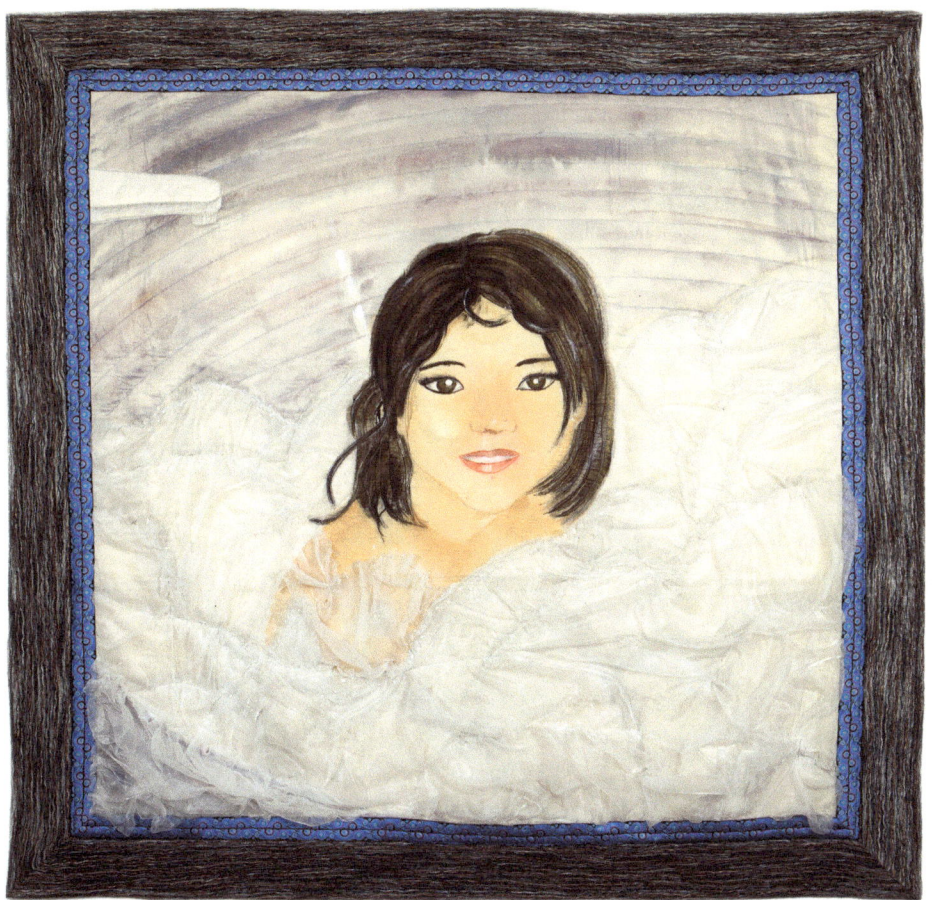

Billings began her art career as a painter, and that experience is obvious here in her depiction of the child. The artist repurposed a veil to produce frothy "bubbles", manipulating the fabric with stitching by hand and machine for a three-dimensional effect. With the current drought crisis in California, those living there might pause before filling the tub for a bubble bath.

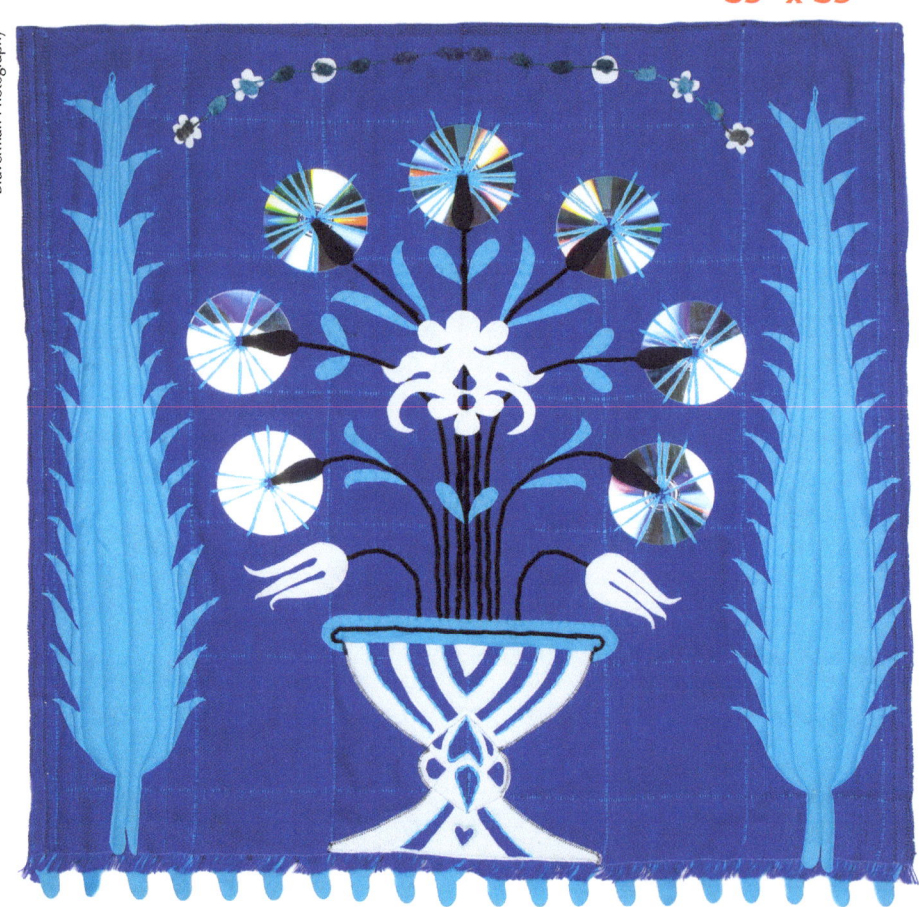

Braverman Photography

MARIA BILLINGS "TREE OF LIFE"

This tribute to the Iznik tile artisans of Turkey, conforming to their color palette of deep blue, turquoise, black, and white, is quilted to suggest a tiled picture plane. Billings's materials include non-traditional burlap, and the reflective CDs are meant to engage viewers in a lively interaction with the quilt.

Photographer: Sibila Savage

GINY DIXON "SIERRA SNOWPACK"

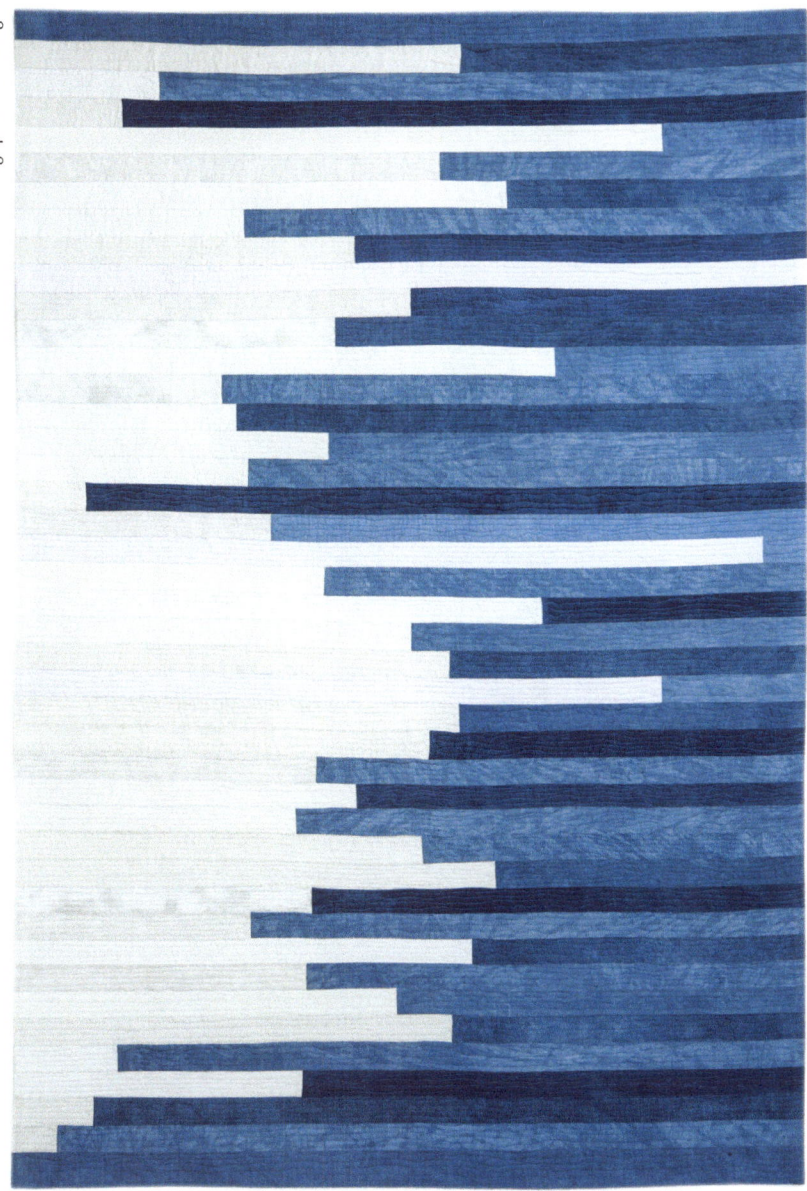

Because water is so crucial to California's ecology, the Department of Water Resources measures the amount of snowpack each year. Dixon's conceptual quilt documents the years from 1975 (at the top) down to 2015, with the lack of snow in many years alarmingly apparent. She created visual variety in the surface by toning cotton with blue woad and selecting vintage linens for the white and off-white strips.

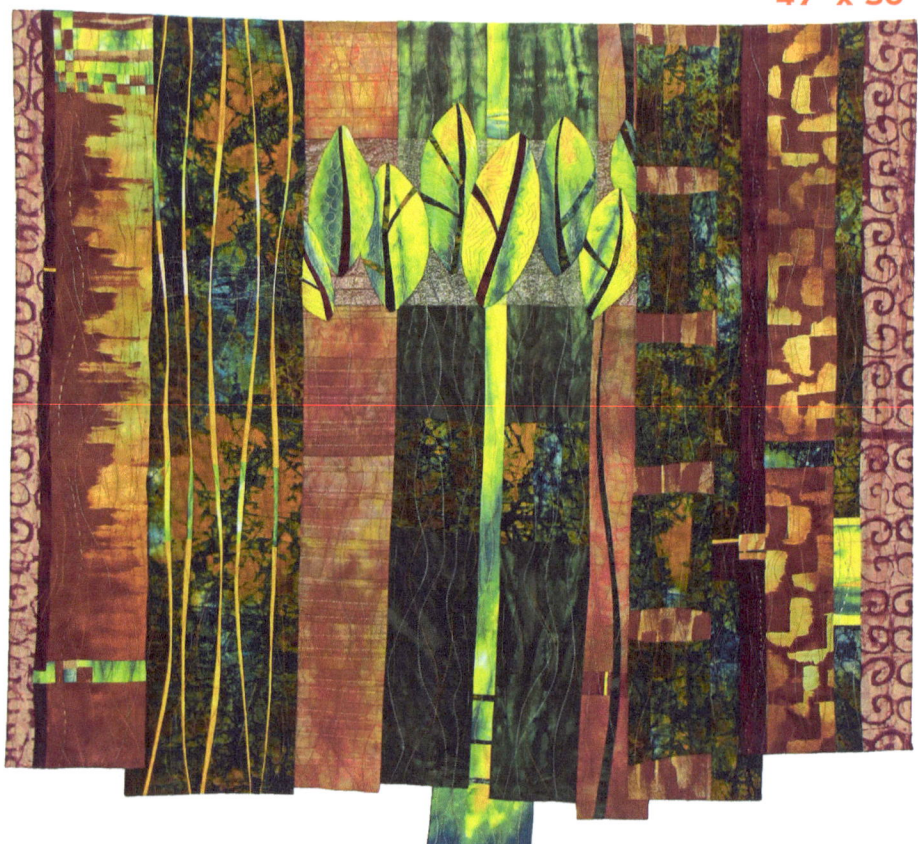

JOAN DYER "LEAVES #3: LAYERS AND TUCKS"

With allusions to the majestic forests of California, Dyer created a quilt whose irregular bottom edge reflects the organic growth of a natural setting. The artist's dyed, painted, discharged fabrics, including one section dyed in snow, have been stitched into a richly textured surface, enhanced by different quilting motifs distinguishing the hues and tones.

MARGARET FABRIZIO "OM NAMA SIVAYA"

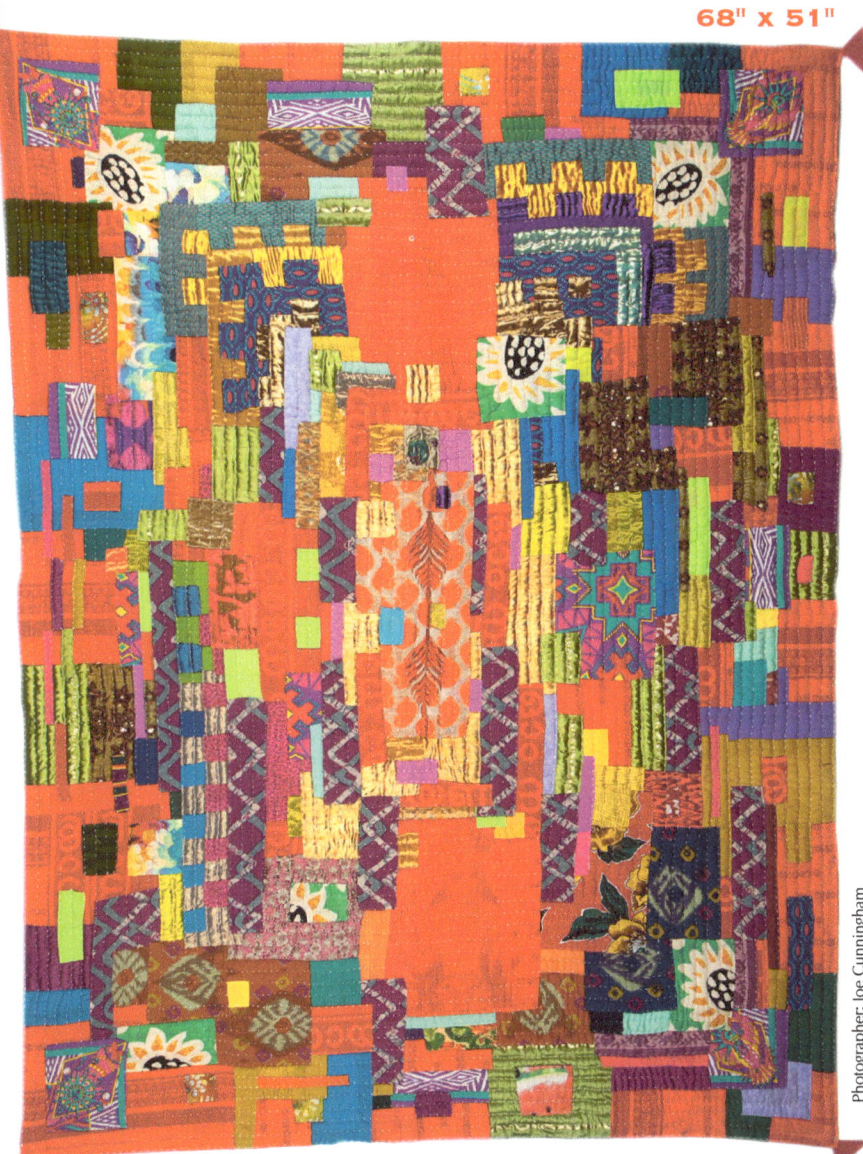

Photographer: Joe Cunningham

Geographically "on the fringe" in the United States, California looks toward Asia. Fabrizio celebrates the goddess Shiva in her quilt. She includes two images of Shiva found in lungis worn by temple priests in India. Her kawandi hand-stitching technique, derived from African-Indian influences, features Indian cotton, silk, brocade, and satin.

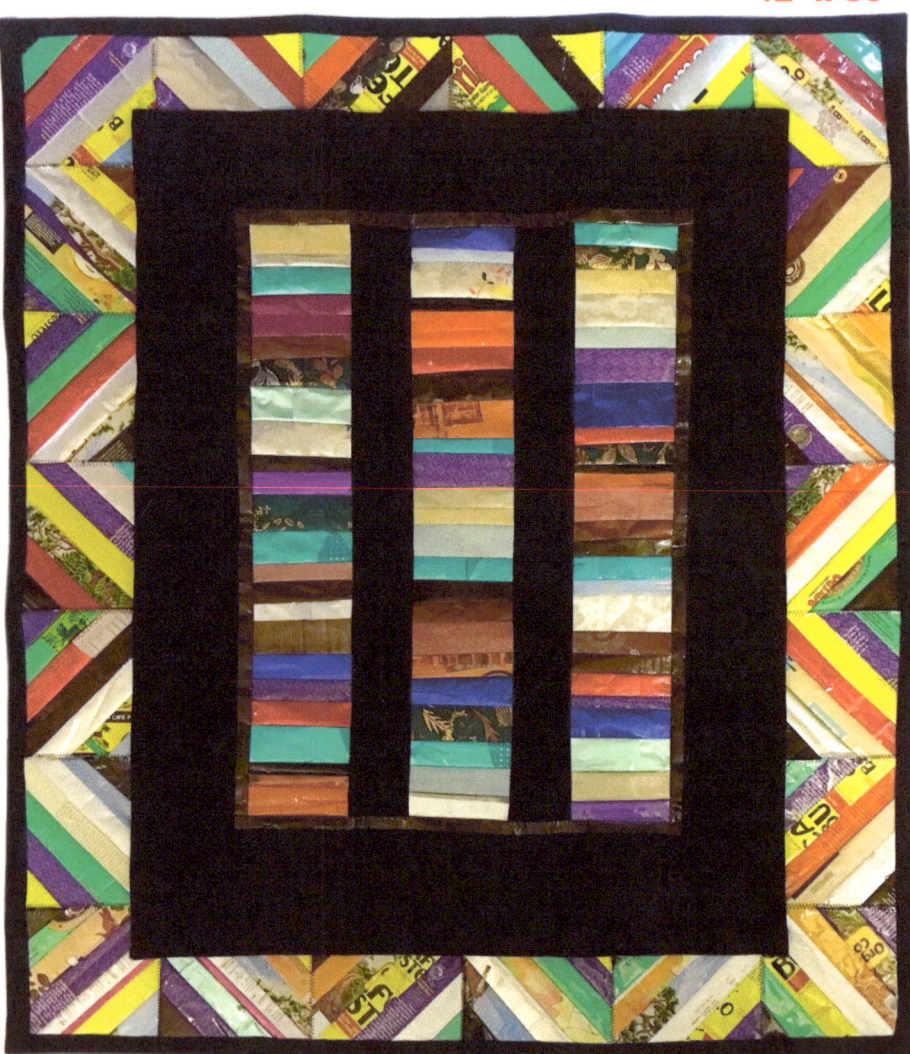

KATHY GRADY "MAKE DO"

Grady challenged herself to use the traditional patterns of Chinese Coins (the central section) and Roman Stripes, with multi-colored strips cut from coffee bags as fabric. Her title, while suggesting the time-honored process of quilters "making do" with what they have, might also be interpreted as Yoda-like imperatives: "Make! Do!"

ANN GRUNDLER "CELESTIAL HIGHWAY"

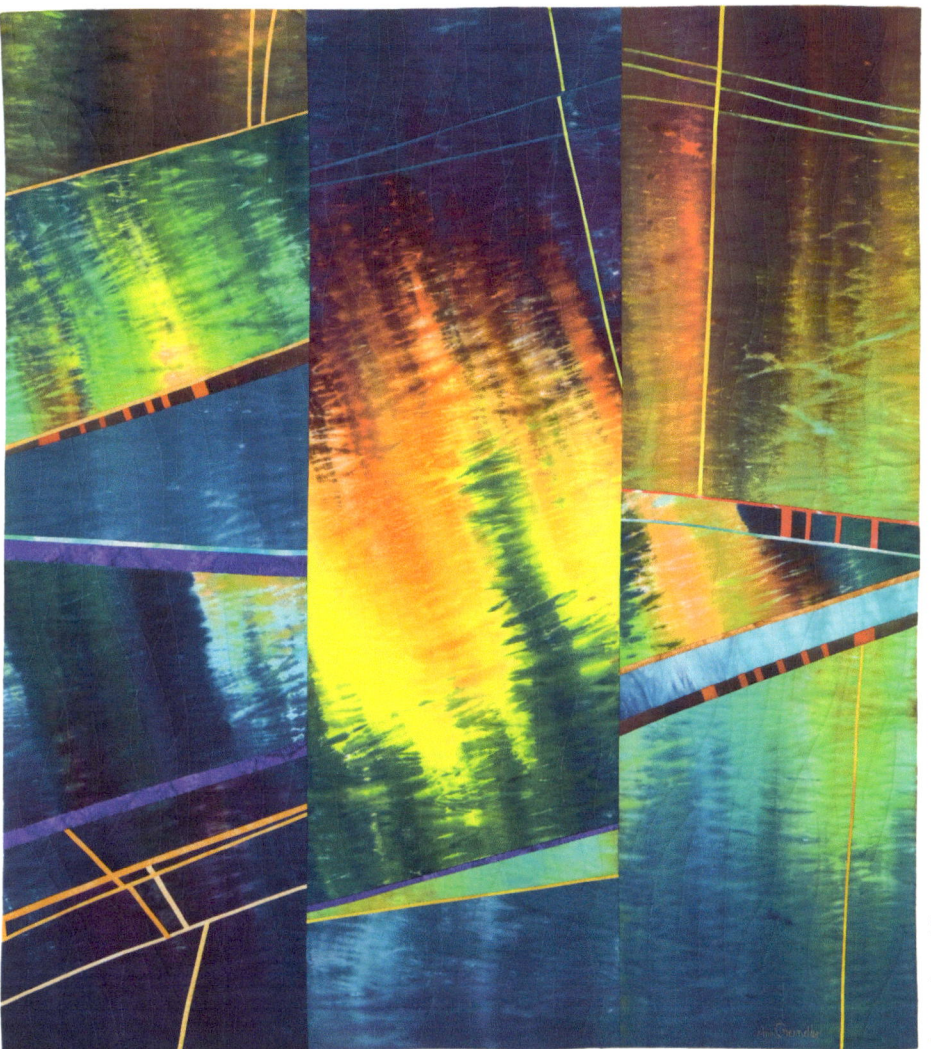

Photographer: Sibila Savage

This graphically abstract work, featuring the arashi shibori dye process, explores elemental forces. Deeply saturated blue may reference ocean coastlines while the central panel seems to illuminate a forest sunset, a stunning vision in California as luminous gold plays against brilliant green.

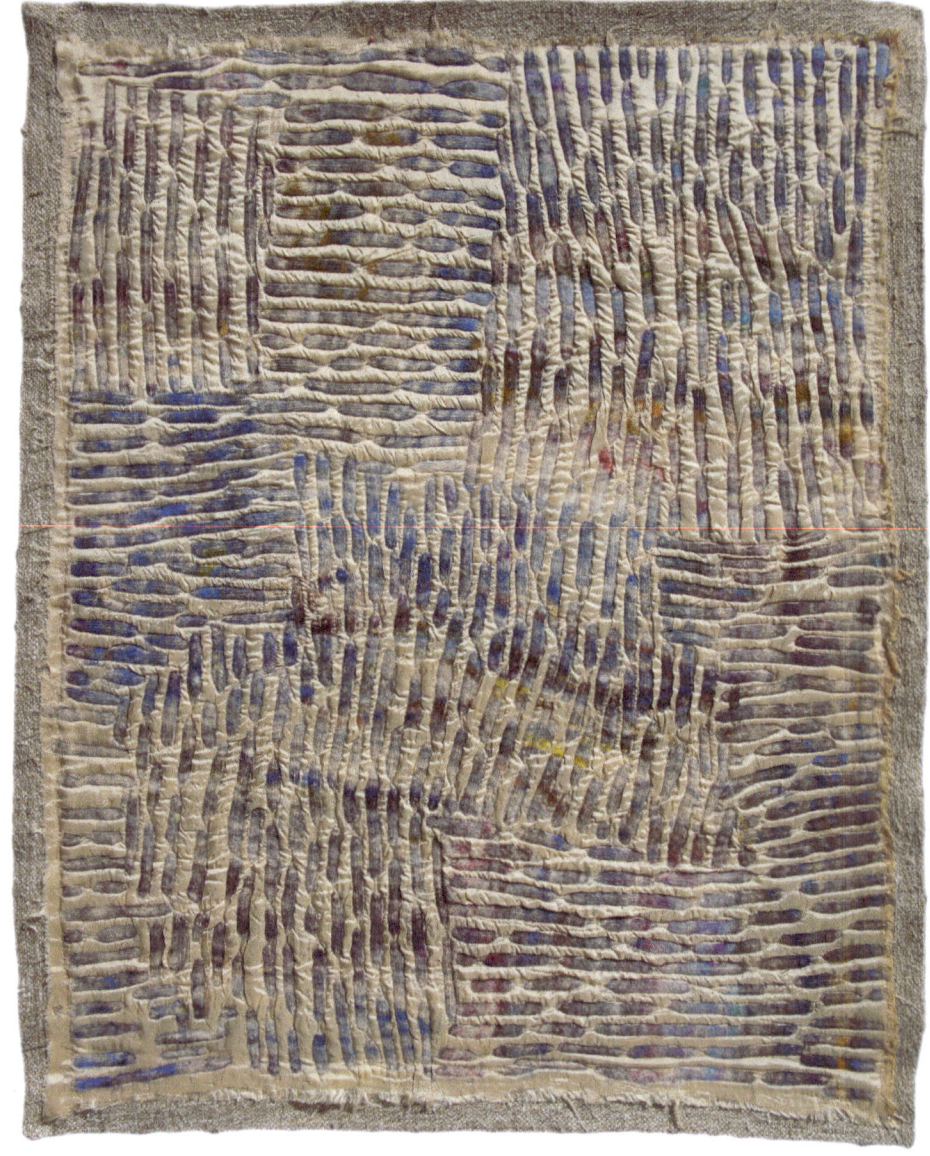

JENNIFER LANDAU "HAPPENSTANCE"

The title of this unorthodox quilt stems from the fact that Landau could not foresee how this surface would develop because it actually was on the bottom during the felting process. Unspun wool, mutely colored, serves as the batting, usually sandwiched in the middle of a quilt. Here it is featured as the top, with the feeling of a well-worn textile.

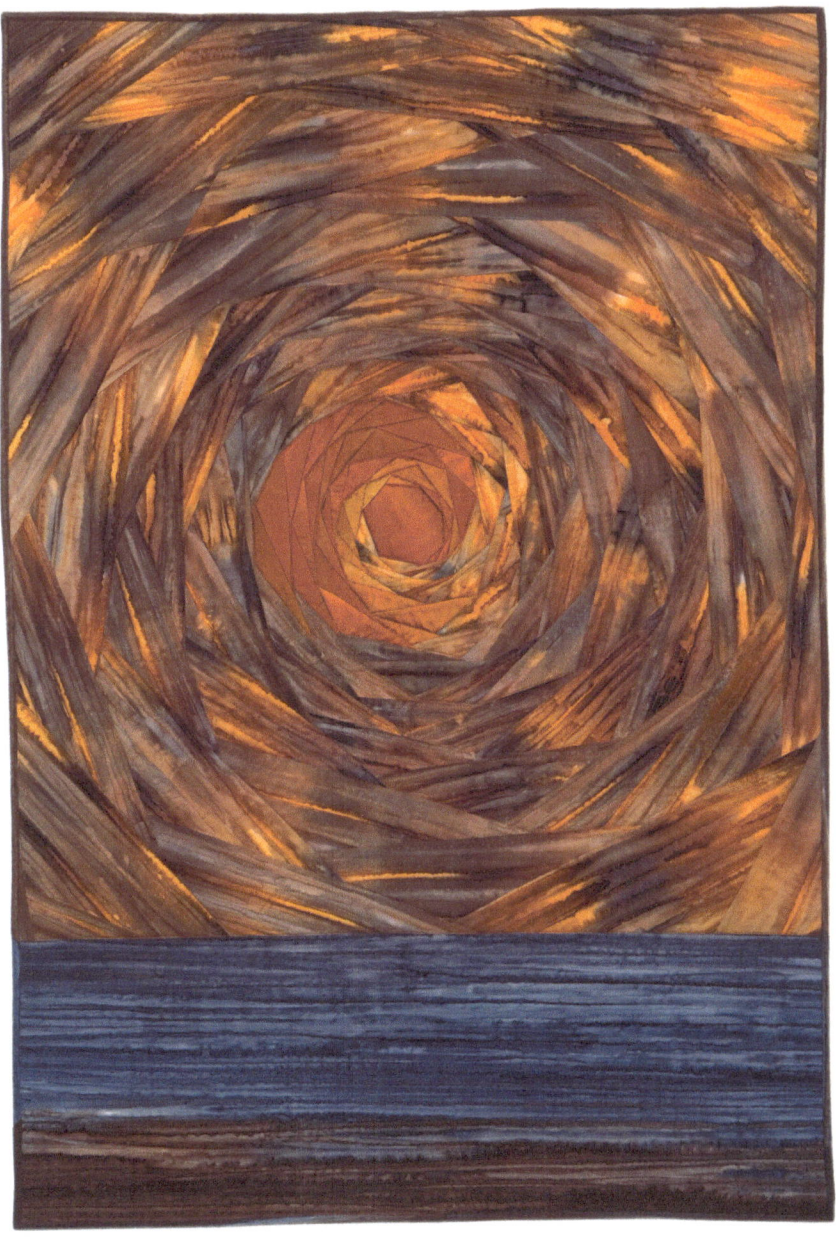

KARIN LUSNAK "CAIRN CHASM"

Lusnak's "extreme" Log Cabin quilt pushed this basic quilt block into new territory for her as she spiraled the strips. By anchoring the composition with a serene blue ground, she emphasized the vibrant movement of the spiral. This hypnotic quilt visually pulls us into the cairn, as if we are looking up into the top.

DENISE OYAMA MILLER "SERENITY"

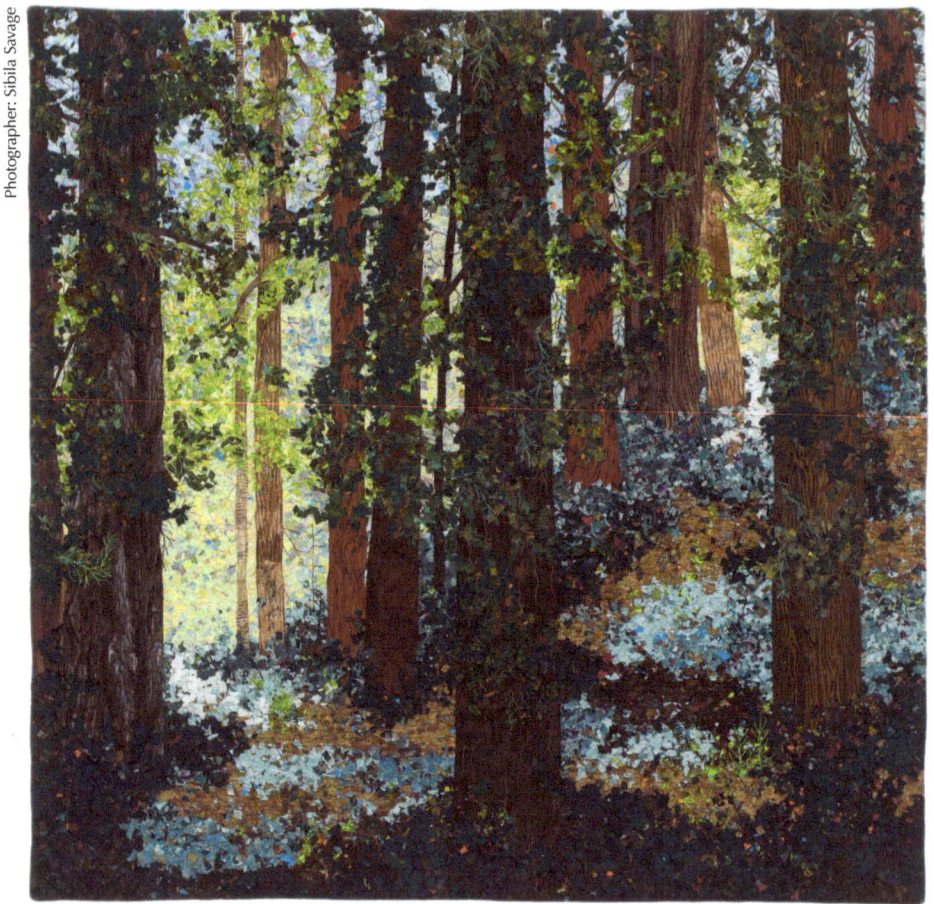

Serenity celebrates the giant sequoia trees in Mariposa Grove, Yosemite National Park. This artist used fabric "pointillism" to render a realistic landscape with thousands of fragments that she covered with tulle and densely quilted by machine.

CATHY MIRANKER "SORTA SONIA"

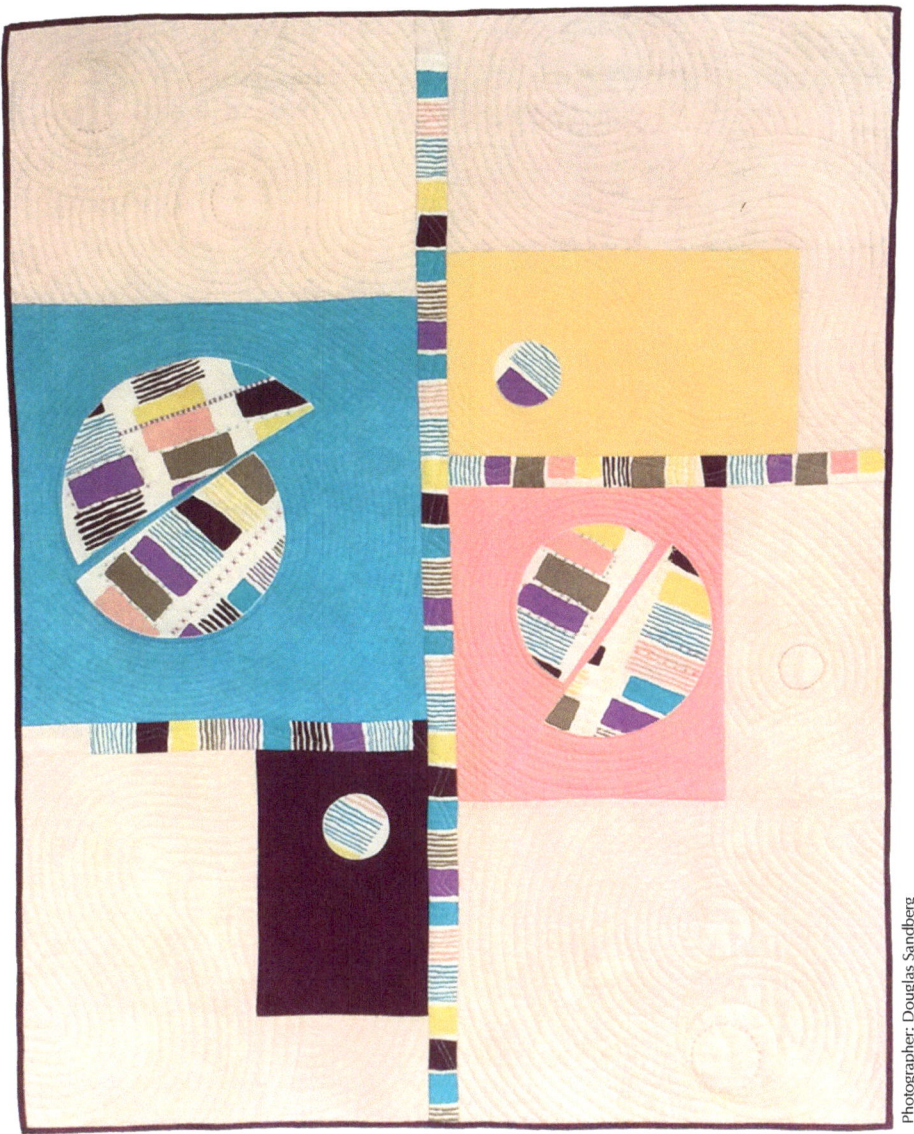

Photographer: Douglas Sandberg

Miranker pays homage to Sonia Delaunay (1885-1979), the Russian-born French artist best known for her textile designs featuring geometric shapes and rhythmic lines. Delaunay's involvement in fabrics began in the 1920's with designs for a silk manufacturer. In this quilt, the artist unified her composition with machine quilting that echoes the circular forms.

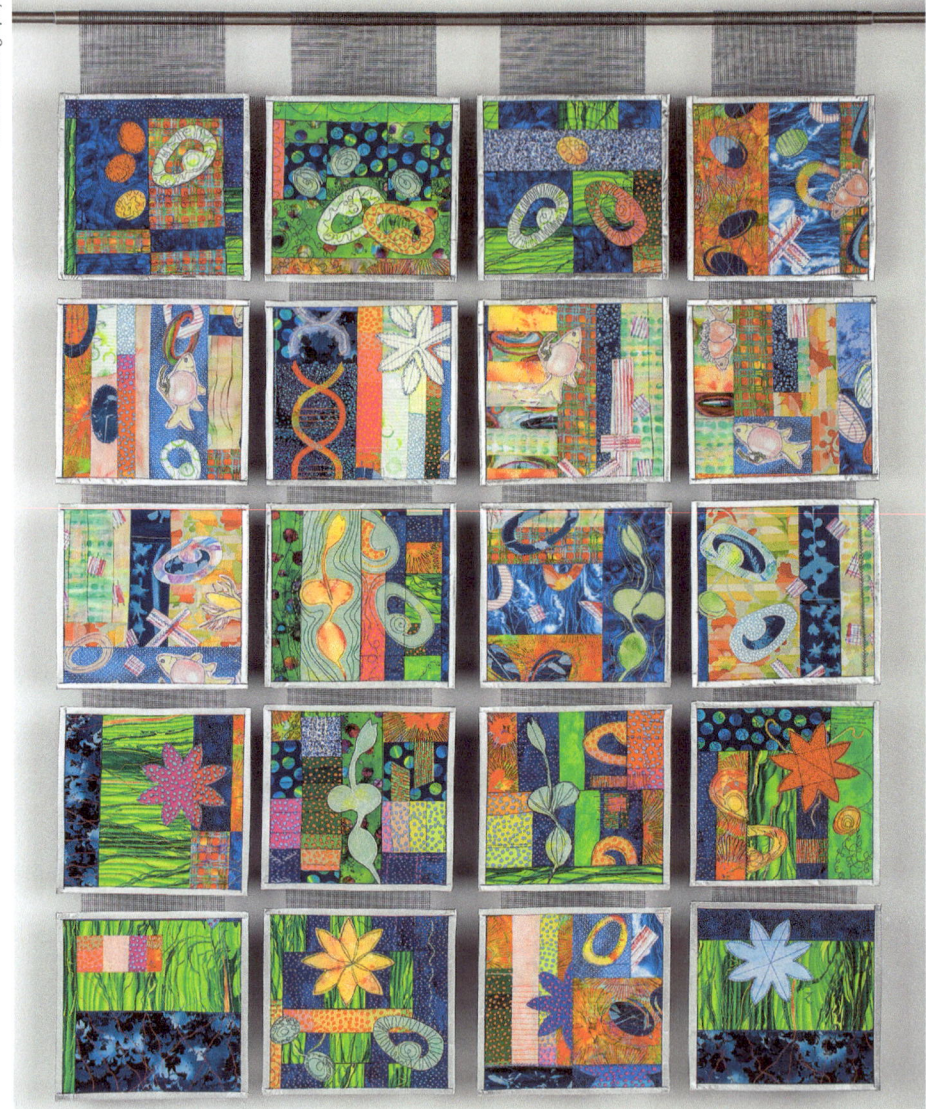

SHARON ROSSI "NATURE MODIFIED"

Rossi encourages conversations about GMOs among those studying her quilt, which consists of twenty sections pertaining to this politically charged subject. Her neon hues seem to reference artificial coloration, and the display system of fiberglass screening hints at the tenuous aspects of any general agreement about GMOs.

NANCY RYAN "SUNSET IN THE SIERRAS"

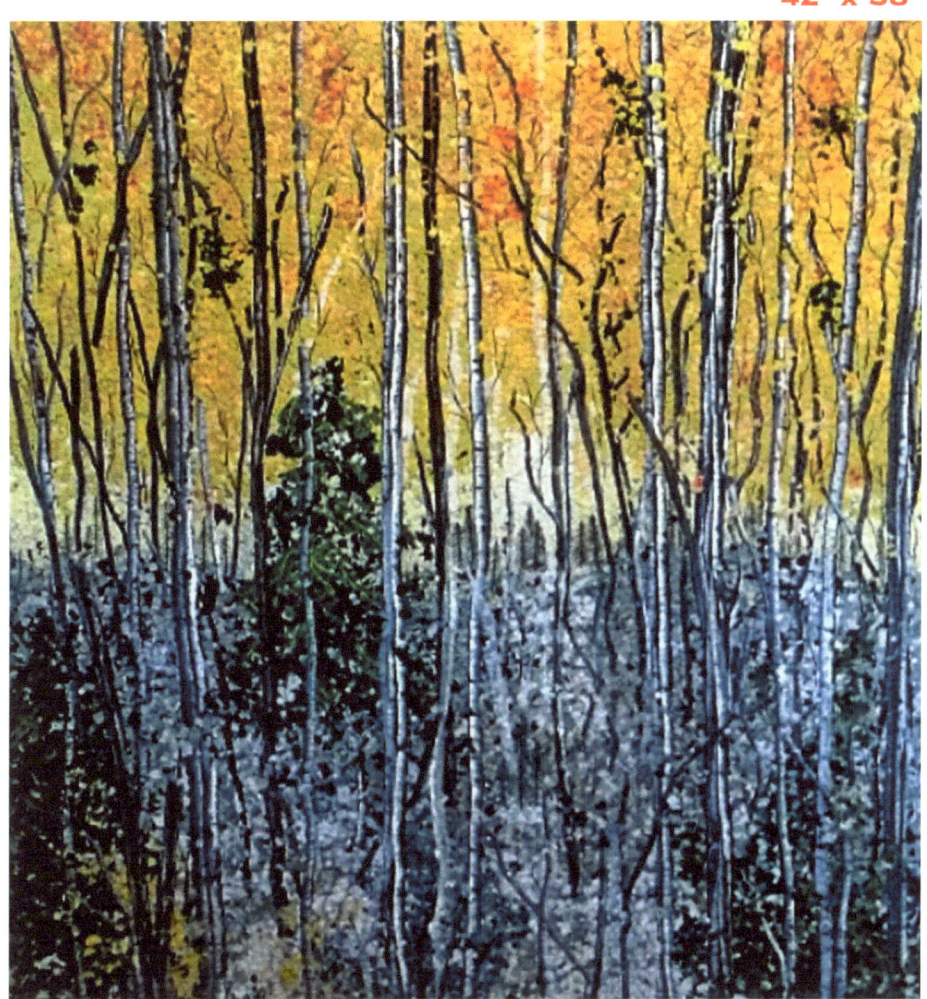

Ryan's impressionistic interpretations of a Sierra Nevada forest incorporate a multitude of fabric fragments, heavily stitched and highlighted with paint. Two evergreens in her shadowy foreground lead our eye into the bright, welcoming background.

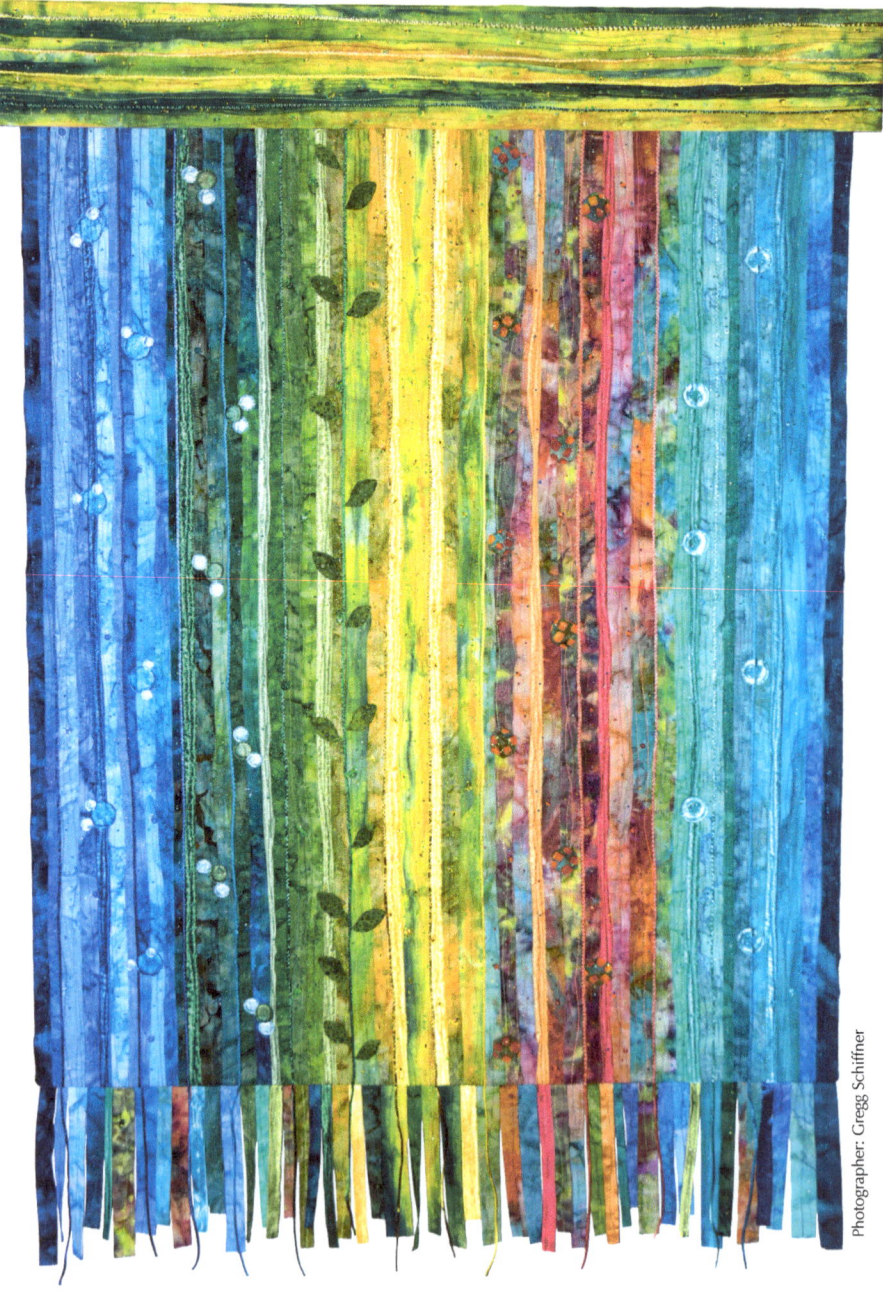

LIN SCHIFFNER "PHOTOSYNTHESIS"

A rainbow of color appealing in itself, *Photosynthesis 1.0* conceptually represents the scientific formula for this crucial natural process that feeds the plant and provides oxygen. Schiffner's vertical bands are in proportion to the basic elements of the formula, and she introduces the molecular structure with painted fabric and beads.

RICKIE SEIFRIED "ENSO II"

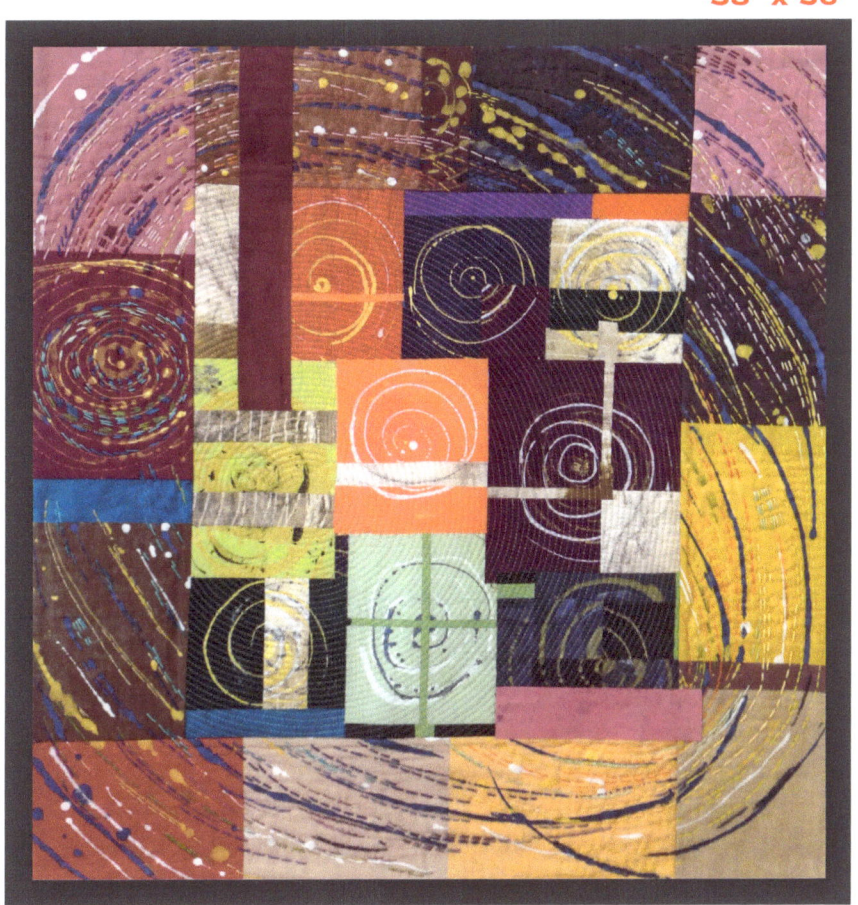

In Japanese, "enso" refers to the infinite nature of the Zen circle, and Seifried closely focused on that shape in the quilt's construction. This maker experienced an artistic journey, experimenting with mono printing and deconstructing painted and printed fabrics, rearranging them into vivid circular formations.

GAIL SIMS "ILLUSIONS OF SPRING"

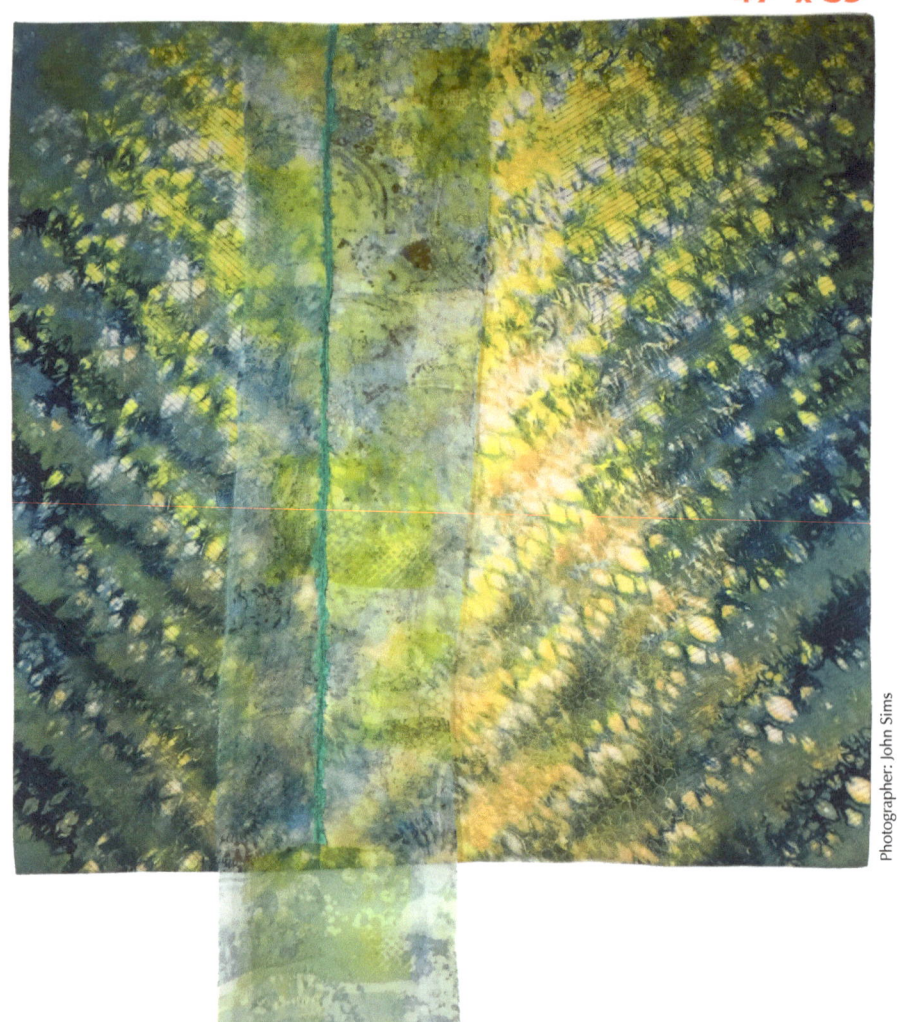

Photographer: John Sims

Sims brings us the idea of anticipation, of that time in late winter when daffodil blooms occasionally are beaten down by rain and snow. Her overlaid strip of organza references the mystery of flowers yet to appear. She created the patterned fabric by dyeing it twice via arashi shibori technique, with the fabric wrapped in a chain. First she dyed in yellow, then blue, producing a soft green hue in places.

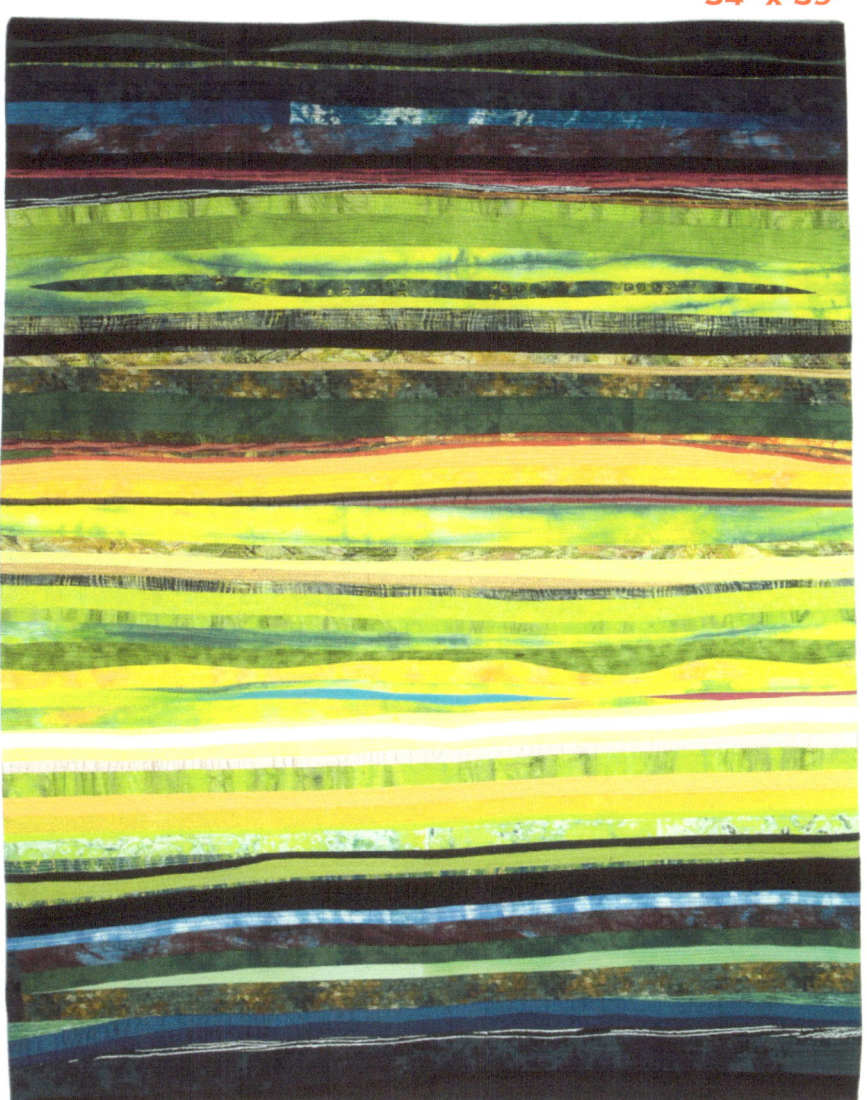

GAIL SIMS "SHINRIN YOKU"

Photographer: John Sims

Shinrin Yoku, or "forest bathing", immerses the viewer's senses in the peaceful ambiance of a forest. The title refers to the Japanese custom of workers going on forest retreats for relaxation.

MARTHA WOLFE "WAITING FOR KELLY"

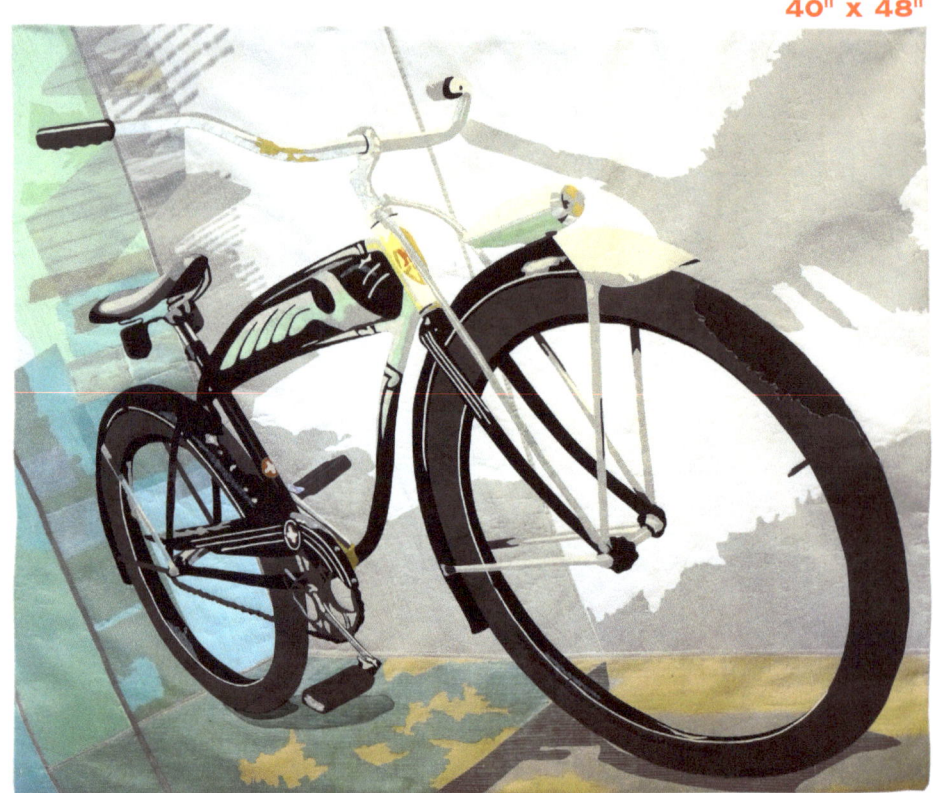

Best know for her realistic imagery produced via photo transfer and raw-edge applique, Wolfe gives us a classic Schwinn bicycle about to roll out of the picture plane as a result of her expert handling of linear perspective. (She photographed the bicycle in a display at the San Francisco Airport while waiting for Kelly, one of her children, to arrive.)

www.ingramcontent.com/pod-product-compliance
Lightning Source LLC
Chambersburg PA
CBHW041621180526
45159CB00002BC/966